The Hard Road

(or Last Year on Earth)

Steve April

The Hard Road
© 2021 Steve April
All Rights Reserved. Printed in the U.S.A.

c/o POB 4331
Mountain View, CA 94040-0331

First Printing
ISBN 978-1-7368755-1-3

A Barberry Book

The Hard Road

Steve April

Also By Steve April

Poet In California
The Weavers
The Sunflower
Scenes From Law School
Birds In America

5 Short Stories

Detour (a novel)

***

Gins. wrote about sex and death
    in an intimate, knowing way,
Emily, the labor and grace of breath
    on any given day, in a silky woven way.
Yeats offered Spiritus Mundi
    on an illumined tray.
        They're all in on the lark,
        they will all be at the séance,
        The séance in the dark.

Hart Crane jumped off the ship
    on his return from Mexico,
Rimbaud journeying to Africa,
    his leg had to go,
Conrad sailing up the Congo,
    Heart of Darkness revealing slow.
        They're all in on the lark,
        they will all be at the séance,
        the séance in the dark.

Charlotte Bronte in her rustic dump,
    penning *Jane Eyre*,
Mahler laboring over his symphonies,
    irregular heartbeat-er,

POEMS OF STEVE APRIL

   Tesla and Parsons draw a spark,
      innovators who dare to dare.
           They're all in on the lark,
           they will all be at the séance,
           the séance in the dark.

***

A performer/showboat not my groove
  Or my public intention,
A dialogue from me, with God,
My major inclination.

An ogre from the swamplands
Wants my music for his trophies,
There's highlands and there's badlands,
That's the way it is.

I have these goldmine shoes
To find the special cleft,
Be frugal my hosannas
Do not have so much left.

You may glimpse the mountain-climber
Beyond the gates of wrath,
In future ages you may pass
His skell along the path.

***

Always open, ogres, monsters
    Stride beside the hills,
Dragons breathe fire on the corn,
Loch lalon, and Loch Ness fills

With slithering creatures and scales,
    Shapes rapacious and forlorn,
Gremlins in the closet chortle,
All your clothes are torn.

Those swastikas in the bathtub,
    Gnats swarm the shower stall,
Who manns that close the portal,
Deluge of killer gall.

Relax, breathe deep, exhale,
    There's no end to the sore,
The doctor with his scalpel,
Exorcise and score.

***

Wild-eyed pistol wavers,
    Settle on rails, bend to crumbs,
Then animate in the branches,
Flutterers, and diadems.

With a tight and black-capped bonnet
    Another sets down in place,
Then there's a playful scrimmage
A breast, a forward pace.

Superlative varieties
    Populate the terrace in awhile
I call them "little darlings,"
And cannot help but smile.

They seem glad to see me,
    However, of interpreter and poem,
They are the lighter and more graceful,
Something in the way of home.

***

'knowledge is found not in skulls but in contact with nature...' Bacon

To understand lightcone, master conics,
    To understand amplification, master
        sonics,
Grok yin and yang, polarity,
To master electricity.
Where there's drive and vision
There's will to form, and mission,
And anyway, a fount of information
Between major parts, a revelation in relation,
Ergo, a mysterious factor X,
No hornbook though to decipher the text,
Though each day more and more by degree
Seems the world fills with progeny.

***
India

A dhobi-wala washes clothes
  For a fee, by hand for you
But you wash your own undergarments,
And hang them out of view.

China

Pay for the hotel to do it,
Though they charge piece by piece it's done,
Coin-ops are rare, language barriers there,
Why go there, when you could be having fun?

Brazil

Laundry machine yes, maids yes,
For $25 per day,
They will clean, cook, and do laundry,
In big cities, same day.

Mexico

Built-in washboards are common,
For scrubbing stubborn stains,
The drawback, uses a lot of water,
Labor involved, and muscle strain.

***

Whose head is in the firmament,
    Whose feet are in the town,
Who spins a web from revelry (himself),
Silky, sliding down?

If papers cry 'Author, Author,'
They are but as fluid rags,
My balloon flies high awhile,
With a modest modicum of drag.

Fresh from dreams the tale writ larger,
Than the labors of Hercules,
Buffo lights are seraphim,
Amen the Pleides.

Waking to a new dawn
One feels the turn of the screw,
A world journeying in time and space,
Sovereign, with a touch of morning dew.

I stood tiptoe upon the hills,
In the mist triceratops, in the past,
Out from the land of dinosaurs,
A lightcone spinning fast.

***

I gave myself up to Morpheus
    That hazy, lazy boy,
For whose infinite smile I long,
    A kindred wind-up toy.

A bosom wide enough for strangers,
Mystery smile on his lips,
Wise brother to Orpheus,
Plucking lyre with bloody fingertips.

***
epistle to hameroff

Laughter, intersection overage grows,
    Between separate bio-river flows,
That coming together in a rush
Cause a superflow in us.

The superflow, too much for our system,
Overflows its bounds in nerve-dom,
Provides an electrical jolt
And inward little lighning bolt.

That causes us a bio-exhalation,
Laughter being our explanation.

Note how resembling quantum consciousness
Super-position, this new Loch Ness,
An emergent quality, and a morph,
A novel chemical recourse.

Likewise, in reverse analogy,
Dreams may illuminate the quantum key.
Placed in a series of stories equally probable,
A creativity burst tubule-soluable?

Then collapsing into a real-world break,
Collapse of the wave-function when we wake?

Superposition and flow in us creates
The dream, and laughter's Watergate.

***
bedroom eyes

Just last night I had a dream
    Two stars shining in the sky
Landed on earth and there they were
When I looked into your bedroom eyes.

When I first saw you I got high as a kite,
And when you put your arms around me
    I knew we would be alright.

Take this longing I have that
    comes on so strong,
Take this pride that
    sometimes gets in the way,
We've come and we've gone
    to where words have no tongue,
Speak to me with your bedroom eyes,
Speak to me with your bedroom eyes.

***

Crackling, jumping off the page,
    Cursive indeed, but seeming electrical
    current,
Romeo and Mercutio collide onstage,
Jumping into unforeseen events.

Shakespeare, Conrad, Dylan could do this
    Seeming in their sleep, the naturals,
Produce more dynamic event than view,
Generate reality's structurals.

'Mama, there's a spider web,'
A tiny tot may exclaim about it,
—Early on these lively cries express,
There's reality, there's games about it.

The little door for kids only
Swings both ways, it is said,
Reality starts out like a game,
With rules, until we bump our head.

***

What is language but a code,
    A code we teach our children,
Starting up more like bird-song,
Urgent cries from robins, skylarks, wrens.

Codes seem natural to an unfolding
Child, a way to communicate,
Wants and needs, likes and dislikes,
New facts, impressions, love and hate.

Birds sing songs, and humans too,
An exuberance, chortling, bodies out,
Language a need, and drive for view,
Luxuries we will not do without.

What a Babel of noises and emotions,
Change 'code' to co-ed, and chaos reigns,
Pluri-potent DNA, stem cells,
Children are born for codes and signs.

***

Beauty came and sat softly beside me
    While I cried hot tears,
I found it hard to thank this beauty
Bound up in my fears.

A broken mirror for reflection,
A past that seemed a waste, so sad,
A future all but foregone, it seemed,
Bitter dregs to taste, to drive me mad.

But time passed, I began to build,
Never wanting to look back,
And Beauty did not desert me,
In fact, she had my back.

She likes to drink the white wine,
I like to drink the red,
To Beauty, who offers me the cup,
I thank that I'm not dead.

***

God come down to guide me,
    Gentle gentle gentle,
Help me find your will,
Your touch imperial.

I tug childish at my bars
When I'm feeling low and raw,
When the world storms my sense's citadel,
And I'm pushed by a cat's paw.

Genetics, purple passion, free associate,
Case study for a detective,
My father murmured in my ear,
"Architecture yes, but defective."

We come unfolding beauty here,
Here, there and everywhere,
And now the stars are folding,
And beauty needs a chair.

***

Morning breaks with new light
    Sifting through the massive trees,
Robust from wispy streamers,
The ground seems on its knees.

Prostrate, wanton, receptive
To powers from the sky,
Step back, are yellows and azures
Much larger going by.

Full throated birds pay homage,
While attending to their rounds,
Or simply gush on with delight
Over the new-born joy they have found.

Do they feel the world turning
In their near unerring flight,
Or part of a master blueprint,
Imbued with magnetite?

***

I keep at my chosen work
    Cause there's gonna be a storm,
To shore up against the ruins,
Give and show a little form.

What comes through me goes through me,
Wish I could turn the key,
A current here, a current there,
An organ grinder with his monkey.

The myth of the starving artist,
A conductor waves his baton,
Much music gushes like a geyser,
I'm vessel, beaten like a drum.

***

To a bird fledgling, leaving the nest,
    Driven is the ache,
To participate in azure,
Eat the sky like a cake.

To navigate through leafy branches,
To catch that sight of bright blue,
Acrobats follow naturally
A destiny in light-blue.

Though many fall out of their nest,
While their siblings fresh at play
Go about their serious business,
A new direction, up and away.

Release at last from wonderful
Unbearable mystery,
Riddle solved, or no more teasing,
Disappearing me.

***

I, I got to climb the hickory tree,
    Rising on the other side of the fence,
You, you got your dreams,
Let's make them come true, overcome resistance.
You feel it in the breeze, you feel it in the night,
The sky's the limit.

He was illiterate,
Don't put him down or judge him by his age,
She, once she was blind, now she can look,
No time to stay in a cage.
You feel it in the breeze, you feel it in the night,
The sky's the limit.

Sure as every mother's child got a song to sing,
Every girl's a princess, every guy's a king.

So I, I got to climb the hickory tree
Say goodby on your balcony,
You, you got your dreams,
I'll bring in the artillery.
You feel it in the breeze, you feel it in the night,
The sky's the limit.

***

I wear dark clothes when I go walking,
    In my old neighborhood,
I got stopped once by a policeman,
Said I, "I'm too old to be a hood."

Does he realize the street signs around,
Near there bear my name?
But April's a month also,
I love them just the same.

Named after my music,
A land developer heard online,
A real estate agent told me,
"Sir, a street's named, your name on a sign."

I assumed then she as joking,
Walked outside and almost cried,
I like to walk by the sign at night,
Though I feel like chicken-fried.

Humble, humble, humble,
There's a wellspring of emotion,
Open up the spigots,
Top it with devotion.

***

I am going to a doctor's office
    Where my heart will do ballet,
A *pirouette*, a *balon*, an *arriere*,
Pas de deux, and roundelay.

Heart, dear heart, beating heart,
Art intimates we feel with it,
A *brise*, a *grand ecart*, a *bousee*,
This is how I deal with it.

Does God peek through the process,
What comes up from the heart?
Wroth our blood we pay the price
Redeem the bottle—art.

Pique, portedebras, fouette,
Avant, avant, avant,
On garde *enture chat*
Ballet is what we want.

***

Kicking humans around like tin cans,
    You get a movie like *The Irishman*.
The fascination with bad boys, hoodlums.

Then at 70, near the ends of their lives,
They look back fondly on monkey jive.
Mean streets, rising out of the slums.

These thugs who signify less than zero,
Given the acclaim while silent heroes...
Find Hollywood royalty to play them.

Show some sympathy for the devil,
Cool cats, pit bulls with muzzles
—And joke about all the orphans and mayhem...

***

I looked for signs in the sky
    While my family ate a feast,
For a flagon in the west,
For a dragon in the east.

Stranger to the earth in ways,
Heir to a lucky seed?
Hardly, success and failure,
A dialogue failing to succeed.

Recovering from a car accident
Hovering there was the trauma,
Face and head affected,
A science fiction drama?

Hermaphroditic sun-children,
Bearers of the kind message-o,
Mermaids flowing outside my windshield,
Jesus Christ, his Imago.

***

Soldiers are muscle, active power,
　　Governments their command-and-control,
Necessary heroes in a crucial hour,
To protect, defend the whole.

On borrowed time we tenants keep
Our bodies, to a degree, in shape,
Subject to e-rhythms, wake and sleep,
Maybe dream about an escape?

Baffled by our possibilities
Whole pluri-potent evolves to an arrow,
Temporary like Achilles,
While our joys turn to sorrows.

Or mellow, gorgeous autumn fields,
Seasons of fruitful harvest,
Graceful enough in time to yield
To death, and the growing darkness.

***

I have restless legs, you know,
    I must journey to the well,
If I do not go walk at night,
I feel like I'm in hell.

The endorphins give a lift then,
And I feel off the shelf,
For God's sake, I feel liberated,
From my cares, I feel myself.

Expand, loosen, abundant bloom,
Walking that mile and mile and a half,
Visions come, my limbs not numb,
I could cry and laugh.

Whitman drinks in the fresh air,
In sync with Blake, heartbeat divine,
Holy night, holy communion,
And drink the holy wine.

***

The pock-marked Instructor
   forget him, man.
Start being the conductor
   with elan.

Mr. Slender Negative
Potapouii, Gus.
Stay within the life-fierce power,
On the rose-blue bus.

Birds sing out a tune,
Sweeping fires are far away,
In another state, a state of mind,
Go your way, your own way.

Breathe deep, relax, exhale,
The end is always near,
Mind shapely, and art shapely,
Do not fear, or tears for fears.

***

Working for *Uncle Sam*,
  The Treasury and Coast Guard,
Deciphering missals from drug-runners,
Agents and spies in our back yard.

With her husband William,
Founders, parents of cryptography,
Our nation vulnerable in times of war,
Enemy code, bombs that wannabe.

Enigma, the Nazi command code,
Purple, the Japanese,
Knowledge is power, Francis Bacon said,
They unscrambled these mysteries.

Dear countrymen, they solve riddles,
And saved thousands of lives,
Sworn not to talk about it,
Their legend barely survives.

The passionate, quirky Friedmans,
Vintage wine their legend guzzle,
Tigers at solving ciphers,
Babel unravelling puzzles.

***

In the prison of this flesh,
　In this porous, sodden mesh,
What chance that wings will sprout,
To help this pilgrim out?

What chance a growing vision,
What hope a sense of mission?
Stranger in a strange land,
With a banana in his hand.

Yet this mesh is also bower,
And this flesh is also tower.
And a reservoir for healing.
And a medium for revealing.

Our cells are awesome, regenerate,
Give us a new lease on fate,
Reach to the stars our aspirations,
United states become a nation.

***

Nero fiddled while Rome burned,
    Is noted in a play,
My body likewise burning down
In an entropic way.

Houses of the Holy call,
Within our heart and hearth and head,
In dreams we hear amazing words,
Cannot remember what they said.

Miracle seems to flicker lightly
Through a tricky mist,
Our awesome moments slightly less
When written on our wrist.

By our scars we know ourselves,
After trauma, we are what remains,
Jesus rose to such occasion,
In moments of doubt and pain.

***

Day turns into night
    Lay your head down, pass to sleep,
Your plans for tomorrow, dear
Let them go, they will keep.

—No more to wake to morning,
Hear a throaty robin song,
Our plans were thin air anyway,
We guessed that—but the gong

Drift down the stream no more,
Or conquer stumbling blocks,
Say "I am" to the water,
Say "I flow" to the rock.

May I linger while you comb your hair?
Music fills my ears, while I'm here.

***

Look outward the dominion reflecting
    Blue sky, green grass, affecting
The inward prism and the riches,
The desire and yearnings, and itches.

The soldier trudges on, ancient cuts
Too painful to remember we forget,
And new wounds give us pause,
Marks of tooth and fang, and claws.

We tread this ground, aspiring,
No way to lose the scars,
A child chorus sings hosannas,
We grow, become who we are.

***

The sky is so big,
    We are so small,
My ears pricked as a hound's
    To hear a Spirit's call.

Feel the flavor burst on your tongue,
    Juicy peach, ripe grape, and embrace
The succulent blueberry,
This is the earth, this is the place.

Ain't it wild that a sim
Can sing a little hymn?

***

My grief is as the Ardennes,
    Scars the Battle of the Bulge,
During periods of turmoil,
A small tincture to indulge.

Don't look back we often hear,
We each have our store,
"A human episode," teases a friend,
Miracles of wonder, miracles of horror.

Genet dreamed he was an alligator,
Burroughs ate a naked lunch,
Gins. munched reality sandwiches,
I've blood-drops on my brunch.

***

Open to my humble inspections
    Birds fly about and sing,
Oblivious to my detections,
    Likewise the flowing spring.

Who am I? Why am I hear?
    I ask God, descend, guide me,
In a humble prayer,
    O to feel Spirit walk beside me.

To have eyes to see, ears to hear,
    What shapes may be revealed,
What banners unfurled,
    What escapes revealed?

Wet with ocean nights,
    Or on a pregnant morn,
Continue with mystery
    The Spirit in the corn.

***

Codebreakers functioned as a team,
    Among them there were code-stars,
Who could crack messages, addresses,
    And orders of battle fast, faster...

***
needs work

Irritation forms the pearl
   In the little oyster shell,
Irrigation leads to art,
   The bucket in the well.

***

There's an anguish for not growing,
   For going round and round,
An anguish for lack of love,
   Even in a wedding gown.

Pains move in, stay a week,
   Others a month, a year,
Afflict the body, spirit,
   To irritate and fear.

What if this lasts forever?
   What becomes of my life?
There's pains that urge you to change,
   Anguish, pain, and strife.

***

Keep the camera low to the ground,
    Babies found in a cardboard box,
Babies crying into a winter night,
    Snowy box with holes to breathe, for light.

A neo-natal nurse
    Who works in a local hospital,
Mr. Ghoul is her husband,
    Don't ask, you don't want to know.

Kidnapped, held in a dungeon,
A homeless girl going, going, gone.

***

Anguish and remembrance, near-naked children,
   Walk to a new school,
So sad, how can they listen,
   Tell the wise one from the fool?

How tell the honest martyr
   From the self-deceiving cult?
Or trust in a saint's vision,
   Or Joseph's many-colored coat?

Slowly, slowly dawns on them
   A new schoolroom in the sky,
What touches a heart of stone?
   And causes the wind to cry?

What brings solace and comfort,
   That most gentle explaining?
Until a new morning begins,
   Done with the complaining.

***

Have you seen the man in the movies?
    He don't cry, don't tell lies.
Have you seen the man in the movies?
The whole town cries when he says goodbye.

Bank robbers, two-bit hustlers,
Outlaw gangs, cattle-rustlers,
Bounty hunters who rode with Colonel Custer.
Waifs wading in across the border,
Hobblin' deputy, drunken porter,
"Mr. Dylan, we gotta hide our wives
    And daughters."

Intermission time, Andy Divine,
Peeps take a peek at next week's show,
    Come to the show.

***

My youth felt like a man-in-rags,
    In a paper bag big tears,
Until I fought my way out,
    At home with my scars.

Take the measure of a bird in flight,
    Or a measure of solitude.
The great arc, the beating of wings,
    A poet in the nude.

Beauty held me for awhile
    Even when I turned,
Then she rolled over in bed
    Until the day returned.

Not much of moment in this,
    Except a river, kind and brave,
When Beauty turns her motor on
    Even the Beast is saved.

***

Elijah walked out into the meadow
    One uneventful morning,
When his chariot came down,
    He departed without warning.
Birds are rarely far away,
Strange things happen over our heads.

Hercules, touched by madness,
    Did violence to his family,
To put the case behind him,
    The labors of Hercules.
Birds are rarely far away,
Strange things happen over our heads.

We want a gentle decline,
    A good death,
We want a hardy going-forth
    How we drew our first frisky breath.
Birds are rarely far away,
Strange things happen over our heads.

***

The butterflies are thirsty, thirsting
    For the nectar in the flower,
The granaries are bursting
    We children of an hour

Turn and turn in spindrift sleep
    While hours pass on by,
Dancing with hyper ballerinas,
    Pas de deux up to the sky.

Seasons blithely turn and turn
    From snow to green and green to snow,
With many colors in between
    On the carousel we go.

—Much like a child on a swing
    Pendulum energy, heedless go,
A dissipation barely noted
    Until the swing goes still.

***

What if this fabulous power
    Resided in you, made home there,
Maybe you could prophecy
    Events in the coming year.

Maybe you could sprout wings
    And fly over the bay,
Or control metallic objects,
    Weapons under your sway.

Suppose you could creep in minds,
    Read other's thoughts, desires,
Or hurl lightning bolts from your eyes,
    And besiege a town with fires.

In each gift seeds of a curse,
Will you save the world, or worse?

***

A female teenage profile,
    A geometry of innocent bones,
More resembling a portal,
    Doorway to the unknown.

At first glance the cipher reads
    Weakness, vulnerability,
The urge to give protection
    To physical fragility.

The bridge waiting to be crossed,
    The riches within, a kingdom craving,
Bearer of the kind message,
    The riches within in need of saving.

Women, men's better halves,
    They who deliver life unending,
Men are defenders in the war,
    Men are their depending.

***

Jack Jack Jack Jack Jack Jack Jack
         Jack Jack Lumberjack Jack
Your mama's callin.'

Jack Jack Jack Jack Jack Jack Jack
         Jack Boy-Jack Jack Jack
Your mama's callin.'

***

Wake in wonder
   Naked thunder,
     And lightning flashing signs for you.

You're riding late out there in your
    Glory machines,
Looking for action, willing witness
    To strange scenes.
A citizen of the world, on a
    Hill of beans.

Coven in the wolf's lair?
You're woven in the loops of her hair.

She keeps you guessing and you're jesting
    About folly and desire,
You're a pilot in a cloudbank, in
    The distance smell a fire,
You're in over your head
    And you hope she's not a liar.

Coven in the wolf's lair?
You're woven in the loops of her hair.

You're in too deep now,
To deep to take a bow.

***

When your stomach says "feed me,"
    And you jones after the meat,
And hobnob with omnivores
When you sit down to eat

How close then to the Wolfman
Who hunts for caged fowl,
And when he doesn't find them,
How he sets up a howl.

Our spiffy cars and clothes,
Giants on this planet sun,
Kings that strut and dominate,
Say a prayer for little ones.

They're part of the loamy loam,
The yin and yang that keeps us here,
The butterflies are thirsty,
Too small to shed a tear.

***
needs work

Crows gather in the snowy skies,
    Darkness falls like a ton of bricks,
We shiver weak and naked,
Without our progress, we lack tricks.

Our skin bereft, no fur or feathers,
Less than a dog or bird,
Even when we crowd together
Without the wheel, a sorry herd.

What is fecund only the first rung,
Here in traffic stop-and-go,
Swinging like monkeys vine to vine,
And learning to let go.

There's a not-so-silent night here,
Enigma stars encode above,
Nature's clues are ever unfolding
Our girls code, give radar love.

***

Music comes softly to my ears,
    Lifts me up, up and away,
A new dimension, through my whirlpool ears,
That holds me in its sway.

Sex likewise a new dimension,
    With so many moving parts,
Memory may bobble and forget
The beat of a touched heart.

There's rhythms for loving friendship,
    For *l'amour amitie*,
Cannot compare to a grand passion,
However, lovely in their way.

Physics speaks of new dimensions,
    Opportunities to grow,
Au natural birds take to azure,
What bird would not go?

A hymn to new dimensions then?
Where we're transported sight unseen,
Fabulous new architectures,
A golden morning, verdant and green.

***

Robins, wrens and sparrows
    Sprinkle in the trees,
Flowers blooming and nature looming
    In intricate degrees.

Highways full of commuters
    Will be dirging edgily gnome,
Buildings full of computers,
    Calculating odds and sums.

Strange to imagine our Witness
    No more a witness here,
Consigned to a world without end,
    The story goes, we hear.

Her first love a brave combat pilot,
    Shot down in WW2,
Married my father, hidden griefs,
    'Don't look back,' and do.

"The Greatest Generation,"
    Dutiful and strong,
Exposed to Depression and world war,
    Learned how to get along.

***
surviving survivor

Some look in each other's eyes
    And lie to their friend's face,
Some go around, and rally the troops
    About who they will replace.

Muscles glisten during challenges
    Sweat pours off shiny backs,
Later, relaxing in the camp at night,
    Production cameras, fade to black.

Physical and psychological
    Gifts and tools intertwine,
In the game of survivor,
    Everyone is fine.

You spend 25 days in sand and mud,
    Punished by nature, yet unbroken,
Until you're blindsided by fellow players
    And a thin man says "The tribe has spoken."

***

In his 50s they wanted Dylan
    To write songs like when a kid,
"Masters Of War," "Girl From The North Country,"
    But he never did.
        Change.
        It's never the same.

Conrad grew older and bemoaned
    His mature work, "Conrad-ese,"
Felt he could not regain adventurous youth
    When hardships came with ease.
        Change.
        It's never the same.

Hearing music down a windy street,
    Or snatches on the radio,
David Roth and Van Halen ruled,
    Where did Van Halen go?
        Change.
        It's never the same.

Rimbaud viewed a meteor
    That "dies behind the hills,"
Human life is like a shooting star,
    That moves until it's still.

Change.
It's never the same.

Our glorious sun causes gravity waves
    Rippling on our rocket ship,
Our event horizon changes,
    Time's part of the trip.
        Change.
        It's never the same.

***

'What holy wine is it thou seekest, son?'
    Dost thou seek machine for universal fun?
That assault with violent levels and degrees,
That the more you kill, the more you be.
Or dost thou seek the marble urinals
Where men talk tough the running of the bulls?
Or that success climbin' corporate ladders,
Where you ascend and leave others in tatters?
'O tell me what this place is where I've come?
A pilgrim long-suffering, long struck dumb,
Folly that comes each day grabs my throat,
I seek humbly the many-colored coat.'
'Ay, folly, folly, offers more and more,
We cry a river before we find shore.'

***

Where be the wine of Emily and Keats?
   Steal me away to where Conrad and Yeats
Talk over dinner of passing gas, a blue bus,
Little things in our society, blown-up pus,
The working mills, industrious illusion,
Industrial mills churning delusion,
Only by passionate inwardness
Even the great sinners do confess
Come clean, imagine a séance in the dark,
Light-footed, and lightly split the lark,
With others of grand company, talk crazy,
And make your peace with eternity,
—Pray the splendid figure of your bride,
Your bird, will greet you on the other side.

***

Have a name like Ritchie Incognito
    That signals entanglements, imbroglio,
Imps masquerade game day, chrome giants,
Sportscasters galumph their pectoral rants,
Then there's a guy who runs an uber church
Gotta kiss his monkey paw, and then lurch
Through the desolation row of golden pews,
Where the privileged store crutches and screws
That turn on the impoverished every day
—Waifs crossing the river flounder and pray
While the bloated golden blob builds his wall,
The greater glory of his moldy balls.
—Hearsay, they crow, cut off the beggar's tongue,
Writhing there on the floor, but written down.

***

Though his bosom more than I can afford
    May I congregate about the sweetest Lord?
I heard a telephone ring the other night
A dear, beloved one not feeling right.
And almost in the same hour stole my breath
An elder dear one at dark door's death.
Too many tears pile on to keep record
To ring the curtain down, tug on the cord,
Turn tongue hirsute to babbling brook,
Break down, shake down, no one will look,
Look forward to anonymity,
Drizzly mist, gray streets, conformity,
Any wild voice crying from the crowd
Pluck tongue with pliers, before gets too loud.

***

Crowns, clowns, vampires, and drug-scarred whores,
　　Motley skells crouching behind each door,
In a theater of lust and debauchery,
The teenage brat-pack and society,
While lost in the whirlwind, rack and ruin
Grows in new souls, slander, vile cartoons,
Drug-fiend spirals and drinking binges,
Golden doors tearing off at the hinges,
Mannikins caught mid-gesture in their lies,
Their eyes of the dead, please close their eyes.
The hallowed theater where ghouls incline,
Where Booth shot Lincoln, now lying supine,
And Bram Stoker hatches fierce Dracula,
And bloody servants attend Caligula.

***
needs work

When you feel the beating heart of a puppy,
    In a basket on Thanksgiving Day, slurpy,
Touch and tug the great chain of being,
How we climb and claw up the slope, seeing
When we attend a memorial service, rooting
For a child gunned down in a school shooting,
Stand shoulder to shoulder with her mother,
Who attends her one and only daughter,
With grief and trouble, anger and soul,
All mixed up in the cauldron, palpable,
—High school boys eat pizza in the back,
Talk about football Sunday, quarterback sacks,
—Kids stream into class, so-and-so looking hot,
The English teacher smooths her dress, parking
    lot.

***

There's a dark side to every one of us.
    Dionysian excess, the breaking point,
   and thus,
Choosing to go down a taboo path,
Or slow meander through the gates of wrath.
Gone the checks and balances, Apollo's light,
With satanic glee embracing savage night.
—Simple as coveting a neighbor's wife,
Killing a husband with a kitchen knife,
The wife interested in insurance pay-out,
Forensic camera popping at crime's lay-out.
Who tells what evil lurks in humankind?
Shakespeare adept describing criminal minds,
The minstrel kicked around will finesse
Heart of darkness up the ying-yang express.

***

Gargoyle, maladjusted,
    Open antenna ears to the universal sigh,
Corrugated, rusted,
    A bright centimeter of anguish, to cry.

Stumbling, fumbling,
    Locked down in self-made penitentiary,
Aspiring, fumbling,
    In your hand a magic skeleton key.

Scratching, lousy with lice,
    Figuratively carrying society's ills,
A sex life on ice,
    Carrying around Pandora's box, what a
        thrill!

Car accident disaster, much to master,
    Dreaming riches, while living penury,
Going to library, where your alabaster
    Love calls will put you in a cell, luxury!

***

Sucking up to comfy professors
   Is not my karma way,
I hear snatches of old songs,
   I do it my pharma way.

—Ho ho ho, a light moment,
   In the middle of dense gauze,
'Sisters fled my confusion boats,'
   Well, just because.

Scars are there upon my head,
   Our passion abides,
The naked and the dead,
   Where our wounds reside.

—While armies march in my brain,
   And go down in defeat,
I wake up the next morning, amazed
   New battles to fight, armies to meet.

***

Crying out in the night,
    A ¼ inch in the cheekbones,
Seen through the rear-view mirror,
    She's grooving on her headphones.

That cipher we call beauty,
    Here in rush hour traffic,
The resplendent, golden quality
    A fortunate bone structure, innocent plastic.

Rolling wheels at American Tire,
    American Sissyphus, I roll my boulder uphill,
During the journey, the need for confessing,
    Make a record, come what will.

***

Isn't there always a desire burning?
    What does the stoned guy with the hoodie
Nodding out in the library learning?
    Wherefor his satisfying peace, and goodie?

Jesus, Buddha, the great illuminers,
    Shakespeare, Emily also hunt desire,
There are so many different world's for hire,
    Monsters and maids, nymphs and bores,
        and liars.

Wherefor the nourishers and nourishing,
    Wherefor the energy of slaves,
To build the golden cathedral, ring the bells,
    Wherefor the courage to be brave?

Every seeker works with hunger/desire,
A few sinners become the saints-in-fire.

***

My body, your mind,
    Strikes a match
My body, your mind,
    A fish to catch,
        Let's make a batch.

Love don't come easy here with the goons,
Some get so much they gotta eat prunes,
If you don't get enough you feel the thirst,
Walk around moanin' and feel cursed.

My body, your mind,
    Strikes a match
My body, your mind,
    A fish to catch,
        Let's make a batch.

Love could be a torture wrack,
When out of joint, you don't get back,
You walk around a high-speed trauma,
A star in your own melodrama.

Please don't desert me,
Why would you wanna hurt me?

***

On your journey to sip from the chalice,
In between the sewer and the palace,
A few may offer you benevolence,
Others rude rebuke, your soft-cheek'd innocence,
Riding, you may meet the joker and the thief,
Starry tales elsewhere told, and told quite
     brief,
—Varied characters will cross your path like
     ciphers,
Madmen or monsters, guides and vipers.
The freak show will focus your attention,
Memory and native apprehension,
The one-armed man with honey'd tongue
Will talk at length and burn his tongue,
Kids exit the funhouse, run the human race,
Saying lover, love is our saving grace.

***

Shunted, cast aside, on a one-way
    Road to sainted oblivion,
A flop at promoting, with a sigh,
    Each day gird my loins, a gift to carry on.

To make one's mark, make a dent
    Or to employ a funkier phrase,
"Scratch the face of eternity,"
    Though that there seems a whiff of craze.

—Insanity to imagine that God hears
    What you say and think and feel?
That you receive special clues at intervals,
    To help you heal, help you keep it real?

Dewy morn summons marvelous birds,
    Travesty, godspeed, answers from the sky,
Let the robins, wrens, sparrows feast on me,
    Nibble my flesh, unto their golden eye.

***

Have to get accustomed to the darkness,
    Darkness that comes before invited,
Not only because it rhymes is there a starkness,
    Cold cases shiver, where day delighted.

Over the houses, cars, bright lights, boom,
Darkness, backing, descending on all,
Gone so quick to nature's sweeping broom,
Or playful premonition, mocking fall?

Life turns serious too quickly, indeed,
    Maybe if in transmigration of souls,
Many chances scatter many seeds,
    Many more morphings compose a whole.

There's more to the picture that what seems,
Where do we go when we sleep, we dream?

***

Waking up from sleep, yawning, yawning, yawning,
Look out the window, a new day is dawning,
Or just before dawn, really, immensity,
Looming, a pregnant pause, a raw city

About to come alive, with cars and trucks and such,
Hell-bent commuters, or from a rabbit hutch
Loosed on the morn, after milk and bran,
Jesus Christ agog, mostly *Life Of Brian*.

We who formed the circle go into
Cycles of yin and yang, charged to do
Our darndest, with exceptionalism,
With social drives, amid our capitalism.

And amid these paradoxes, round and round,
We spin, like pathologic tops, rebound.

***

Flashes of genius,
    And creative blocks,
The boy who draws circles
    Wants to eat the clocks.

A touch of autism,
    A modest little hymn,
The start of a howl
    That rises in him.

Let desire be my ship,
Awe unfurl my sails,
Though my sanity in question,
And my ciphers braille.

Run your own race, do not compare,
That way lies madness, arrested gesture, beware.

***

Life is no simple walk in the park,
    We each apparently require
Our unique, identifying mark,
To return to, inspire, and aspire.

Our own magnetic, musical itch
That opens our arms to what gives,
Our heart too, our conscience, our inner core,
A consciousness hungers to live.

All the riches that the world offers
Are enough to make a grown man cry,
And society's child, so forlorn and little,
There's the cleft, to live or let die?

Should I want more, in touch with my greedy?
Or orphan, fly free, multi-dimensional seedy?

***

There's mental pain, stress, anxiety,
 Or pain from loss of God, eternity,
There's physical pain, an organ on the ropes,
Or finding, then losing, with loss of hopes.

Pain sharp or dull, intense or mild,
Genet's pain, a monster and a child,
Pain that bears down, you feel there's no end,
Or seems a friend, when you're on the mend.

—A part of life, easy come, easy go,
Stiff upper lip, relax, keep your cool flow,
—Or pain that grows slowly and builds
In intimate places, forms a guild

Until you are dealing with unions of pain,
United they stand, the pain remains.

***

Atop the mountain looking down one day
Thankful to be here, woofing on my way,
Wheels on wheels revolving below my ken,
Body, mind and spirit close again.
Ciphers on ciphers, sky with flashing lights,
The glorious stars, that beckon in the night,
Our language, social discourse, codes and veils,
Our bodies send us signals through our cells,
Private vats, ours to protect and guard,
The "A"s and "D"s on a child's report card,
—Our privates from outside with a shield
Without ciphers, DNA, clods in a field,
Why then feel bizarre in this bazaar land?
A stranger trip than we can understand.

***
'the hard road'

My sister's language is inflammatory,
  In pain, her verbiage derogatory,
My brother makes Hollywood jokes,
Wheels are falling off, but not the spokes.
  There I go carrying my load
  On the hard road.

After all love's flavors he tasted
Don Juan wonders on what's wasted,
Another friend works in a bank,
Says days spent there remind him of a tank.
  There I go carrying my load
  On the hard road.

Our grasp is great, but reach goes further,
From saving lives to bloody murder,
From the raw earth we come, not melody,
Day after Thanksgiving threnody.
  There I go carrying my load
  On the hard road.

***

Morpheus, idyll of sleep,
    Mischievous smile on his lips,
Soft, round, mellow belly,
Blood-red nails on his fingertips.

Into your bosom please commend us,
From the jungle, the x-creep, the stew,
With loftier aspirations
To wake up fresh and new.

Mend thou our ravaged skeletons
With your magic skeleton keys,
Enfold us in your bosom,
Playing piano with black keys.

That we recharge our batteries,
Rise at peace with God and man,
A healer science will yet explain
With experimenting, if they can.

***

Enemies look at the back of my head,
    Ex-lovers hide under my bed
      In my dark hours,
Ladies who've never loved before
Invite me in through their door
      In my dark hours,
In my dark hours, you are there for me,
In my dark hours, you're the light I see
      Sometimes anyway, sometimes anyway.

Dark eyes looking out under hats,
In the marketplace I'm getting fat,
      In my dark hours,
Car crash in the rear-view mirror
Down by the river,
In my dark hours, you are there for me,
In my dark hours, you're the light I see
      Sometimes anyway, sometimes anyway.

When there wasn't a prayer,
When they sucked up the air,
All of our days, feeling your way to love me,
When I couldn't see the sun,
Thought I'd lost everyone,
Always loved you anyway.

Your brother will be back again
Though it's rainin' on Crestwood Lane,
Drifting down the window plane, on Crestwood
    Lane,
They're baking bread and chopping wings,
    while the bluebird sings,
Still life goes on much the same, on Crestwood
    Lane.
Your brother will be back again,
Though it's rainin' on Crestwood Lane,
Drifting down the window pane, on Crestwood
    Lane,
They're baking bread and chopping wings, while
    the bluebird sings,
Still life goes on much the same, on Crestwood
    Lane.

POEMS OF STEVE APRIL

***

East to the dawn we go, it's a long trip,
    Sailors and passengers on a great ship,
Will it all be revealed in the next clip?
The ones you know and the ones you don't know,
    east to the dawn.

The word's goin' round, there's a room to spare,
A dollar a day, gotta work your fare,
Go east young man, better grow your hair,
Birds of paradise, work and money's there,
    east to the dawn.

They're wavin' and screamin', there at the gate,
Brothers and sisters and those on a date,
Beautiful strangers thrown together by fate,
They will set sail before the day is done,
    east to the dawn.

Everybody's laughin', everybody's singin',
Open your hearts to enjoy,
Everybody's happy, all the girls and boys
    'open their hearts to enjoy.'

East to the dawn we go, it's a long trip,
Amelia Earhart's children on a great ship,
Dolphins will swim ahead, it'll all be hip,

The ones you know, and the ones you don't know,
> east to the dawn.

You wake to music, from ship to the shore,
Prophetic sounds at perception's door,
You wanted wisdom but they gave you a cure,
> east to the dawn.

About the Author

Steve April is a retired teacher and (former) attorney. He resides in Mountain View, California.

Steve's first book Poet In California (1992, 2003) received positive commentary from two National Book award winners, a Pultizer Prize winner, and the current U.S. Poet Laureate.

Gerald Stern a National Book award winner says, "Poet In California is a fine book that reaches for the absolute without shame, and with art. It benefits, if anything, from your separation—apparent—from schools and movements. I wish you the greatest luck. I will continue to read you." Rachel Hadas, Distinguished Professor at Rutgers says, "I thought of Rilke, Whitman, and some of the Modern Greek poets I admire..." Pulitzer Prize winner James Merrill says, "Poet In California has many beautiful moments." Charles Guenther says, "An extraordinarily fresh and vibrant collection...showing the best heritage from the Surrealists and Pound/Eliot." Joy Harjo, our U.S. Poet Laureate says, "I'm glad you're out there working on the questions that baffle and inspire all of us."

www.ingramcontent.com/pod-product-compliance
Lightning Source LLC
Chambersburg PA
CBHW060208050426
42446CB00013B/3026